Marie Antoinette and Her Lavish Parties

The Royal Biography Book for Kids
Children's Biography Books

BABY PROFESSOR
EDUCATION KIDS

Speedy Publishing LLC

40 E. Main St. #1156

Newark, DE 19711

www.speedypublishing.com

Copyright 2017

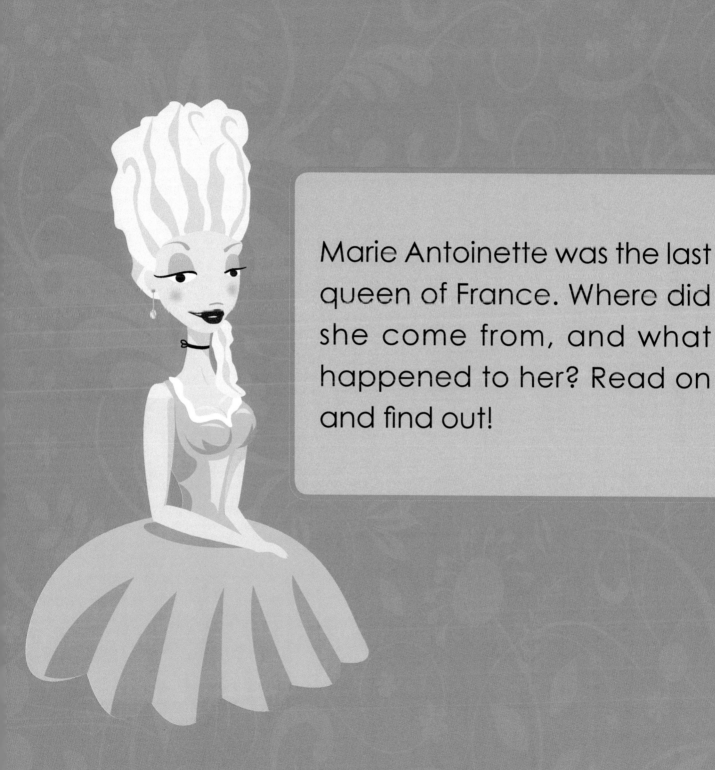

Marie Antoinette was the last queen of France. Where did she come from, and what happened to her? Read on and find out!

The Lovely Young Queen

Marie Antoinette was born in 1755 in Austria. She was of the Austrian nobility, and when she was 15 she married Louis, who would become King Louis XVI of France when his father died in 1774. This made Marie Antoinette the Queen of France.

MARIE ANTOINETTE

When Marie first came to France, she was very popular. She was pretty and young, and everyone from the nobility down to the peasants thought she was a great addition to the royal house of France. Politicians also thought the marriage helped keep Austria friendly with France, so they liked the young queen for that reason.

The World of the Very Rich

The France that Marie Antoinette came into was divided into a small group of nobility and wealthy landowners, who held most of the power and money in the country, and the great mass of peasants and laborers. The Catholic Church was also a powerful force, and some of its bishops lived a life very much like the life of the nobility.

UPPER CLASS FAMILY

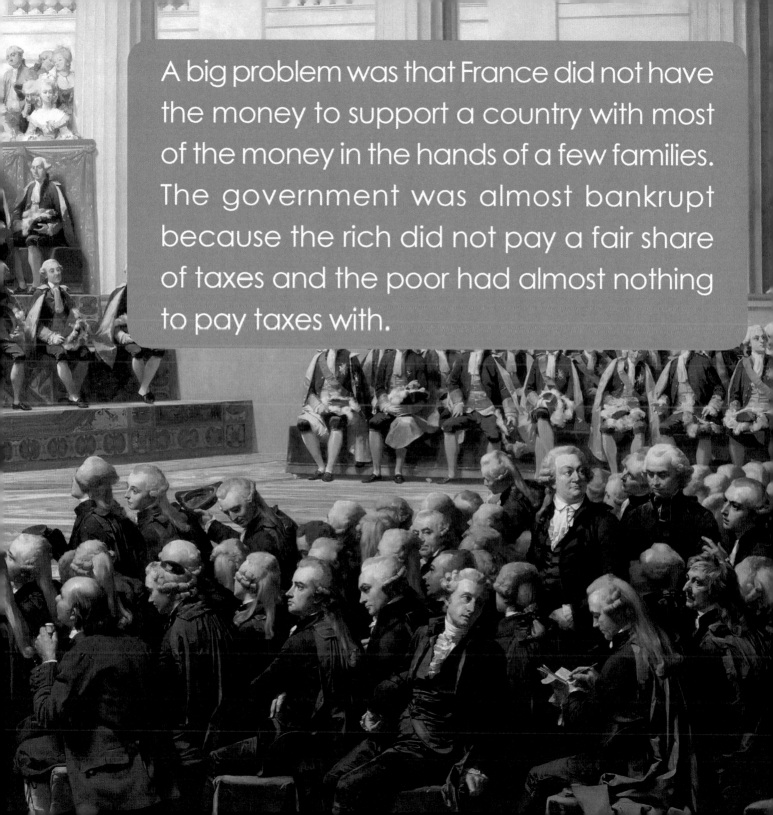

A big problem was that France did not have the money to support a country with most of the money in the hands of a few families. The government was almost bankrupt because the rich did not pay a fair share of taxes and the poor had almost nothing to pay taxes with.

Years of bad weather led to many crop failures, and this made even the most basic food expensive and hard to get. Peasants paid more than half their income just for bread and other basics, while the rich had dinners of strange delicacies brought from distant lands.

WOMAN SELLING AT THE MARKET

FRENCH ROYAL FAMILY

Marie Antoinette came from a wealthy, powerful family in Austria, and joined another wealthy, powerful family in France. She expected a life of luxury, delights, and leisure.

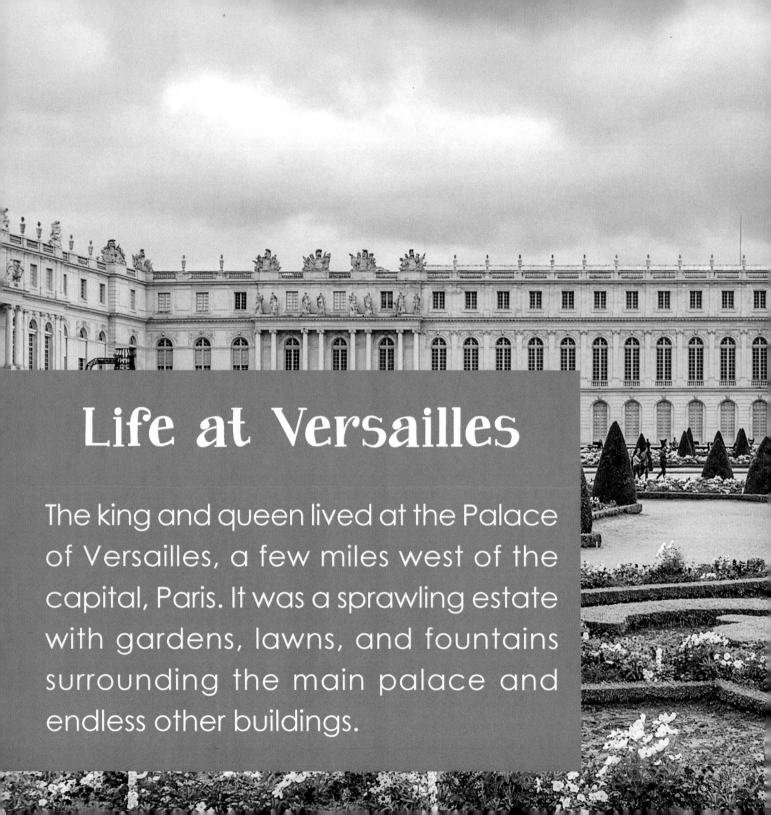

Life at Versailles

The king and queen lived at the Palace of Versailles, a few miles west of the capital, Paris. It was a sprawling estate with gardens, lawns, and fountains surrounding the main palace and endless other buildings.

There were grand ballrooms and small salons, extravagant bedrooms, and intimate places where people could sneak away and get to know each other better.

ORANGERIE DE VERSAILLES

All the effort at Versailles was to provide pleasure for the king, the queen, and the courtiers, and to impress visitors from other lands. All this show required hundreds of servants, cooks, dressmakers, gardeners, musicians, cleaners, and bakers of fancy cakes, not to mention guards and people to take care of the horses.

Running Versailles was hugely expensive, and the royal family did not pay for it. Most of the money for Versailles came from the taxes the government took in. And the taxes that were spent on fancy suppers for the king and queen were not available for paying for hospitals, or to repair roads, or do the other things the country needed.

CEILING IN THE PALACE OF VERSAILLES

The Work of Pleasure

Versailles existed to give pleasure for the royal family, and the royal family worked hard to enjoy it. The queen usually slept in until noon or later, because she might have been partying late into the night. Then she dressed and ate, and went out to enjoy the palace grounds for a few hours before the next set of grand events began.

The king was less of a party person than the queen, and often rose earlier and went to bed earlier than she did. They slept most of the time in separate bedrooms far apart from each other in the palace. This let Marie Antoinette concentrate even more on the hard work of having scandalous fun.

SMALL APARTMENT OF THE KING IN THE PALACE OF VERSAILLES

Parties

The palace staff competed to see who could think up and put together the most astonishing and glorious parties. There were masked balls, where everybody wore masks and pretended not to recognize everybody else, so they could be as daring and scandalous as they liked. There were formal balls, with courtly dances and endless music. There were costume parties, where people dressed up as mythological gods and heroes, or people from French history.

TABLE WITH LOTS OF FOOD

Food

All of the gatherings, not just the parties, involved lots of food. There was always far more than the people present could eat, so a lot of the fine food was wasted. Chefs used the rarest ingredients and the best cuts of meat to delight the palates of the rich, while just a few miles away poor children were going to bed hungry for the lack of basics like bread.

Clothing

Not just for parties, but every day, the queen and the people at court wore the finest materials cut to the latest fashions. Teams of clothing designers and seamstresses worked hard to prepare remarkable outfits that would show off the queen and other people at court to the best advantage. Some of these clothes were only worn one time.

FRENCH FASHION

THE PETIT TRIANON

Playing Pretend

The king built for the queen a model farm, Le Petit Trianon, on the grounds of Versailles. There the queen and her special friends could go and play at being milkmaids and shepherdesses. Of course other people actually took care of the sheep and cleaned the farm buildings, but Marie Antoinette and her friends got to wear cute outfits and flirt with gentlemen of the court who dressed up as shepherds, hunters, and farmers.

Gambling

The court in general was addicted to gambling, often for very large sums of money. A man or woman might win or lose, on a single hand of cards, more money than a whole peasant family might see in ten years of hard work.

MEN AND WOMEN PLAYING CARDS

MASKED BALL

The Best of Everything

In short, if there was some pleasure, it had to be present for the royal household to enjoy, and in the very best form possible. Nobody seemed to care how much it cost or where the money would come from, as long as the people at Versailles were enjoying themselves.

The Queen's Scandals

Although the queen was much loved when she first came to France, her reputation suffered as word of the way she lived got out. Rumors spread about wild events at Versailles. Some were accurate reports, and some were made-up stories, but people had lost their love of Marie Antoinette and became ready to believe the worst of her.

WOMEN PROTESTING

QUEEN MARIE ANTOINETTE AND
TWO OF HER CHILDREN

Here are some of the most serious scandals that hurt the queen's reputation:

Who is the Father?

There were rumors of love affairs at the court, not just among the courtiers and other nobles, but at the highest levels. People said that Marie Antoinette had taken a foreign diplomat as a lover, and that at least one of her four children was not the king's child. There was no proof of this rumor; but rumors like this, once started, far outrun the need for proof.

The Diamond Necklace Affair

In 1785, Marie Antoinette was the victim of a plot by a countess. The countess convinced a high church official to give her a very expensive diamond necklace, saying that the queen wanted it. The official did this in hopes he could join the circle of the queen's closest friends. But the countess took the necklace to England and sold its diamonds for herself.

COLLIER REINE BRETEUIL

MARIE ANTOINETTE ON TRIAL

Marie Antoinette had nothing to do with this scheme, and was more a victim than a thief. But people generally thought she must have had a hand in the plan somehow, and her reputation suffered even though the countess and the official were the ones who had done wrong.

Let them

eat cake!

PEASANT FAMILY

People were starving throughout the country because of a crop failure and the high price of bread. The rumor went around that the queen, when she was told that people could not afford to buy bread, merrily said, "Then let them eat cake."

This is perhaps the one thing most people know about Marie Antoinette, although she probably never said the words. By this time, 1789, people were fed up with the king and queen and would believe any bad thing they heard about them.

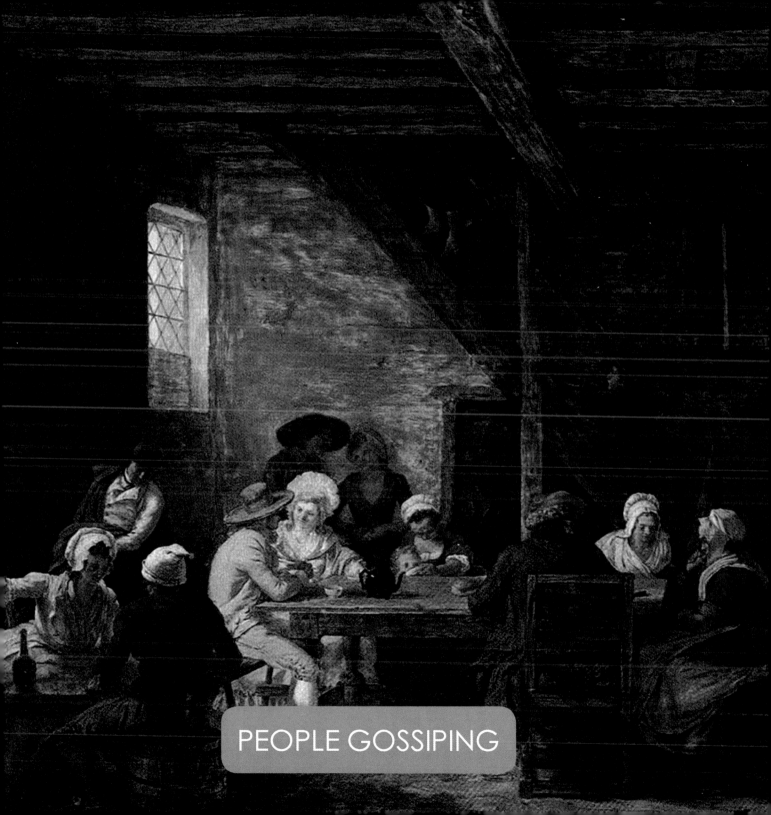

PEOPLE GOSSIPING

FRENCH REVOLUTION

The End of the Queen

In 1789, as the French Revolution started, there was a march on Versailles to protest the lack of bread and to convince the king to move back to Paris. This was the end of Marie Antoinette's glamorous life at Versailles.

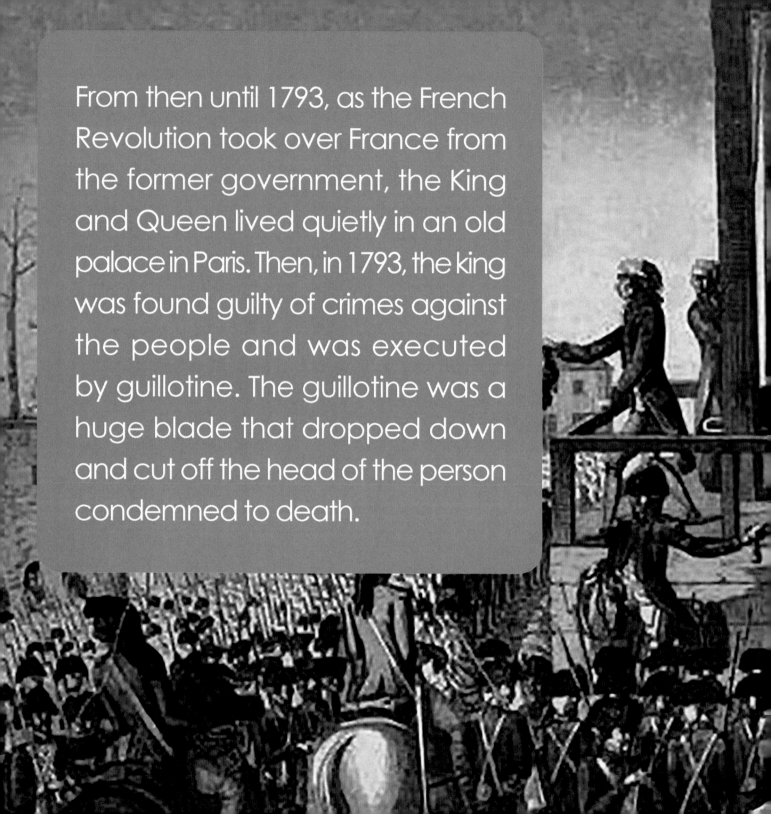

From then until 1793, as the French Revolution took over France from the former government, the King and Queen lived quietly in an old palace in Paris. Then, in 1793, the king was found guilty of crimes against the people and was executed by guillotine. The guillotine was a huge blade that dropped down and cut off the head of the person condemned to death.

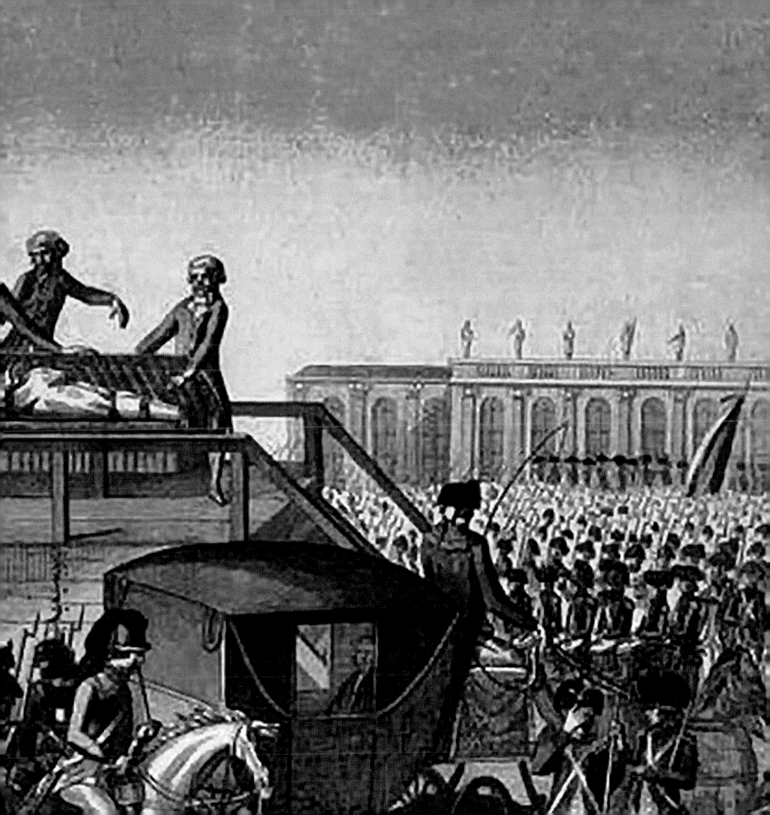

MARIE ANTOINETTE EXECUTION

Marie Antoinette died the same way, about nine months later. She had gone from being a symbol of fashion and glamor to a symbol of all that was wrong with the nobility and the old way of governing France.

Learn more about the French Revolution

The French Revolution was a time of danger, excitement, and great changes for France. Learn more about these times from Baby Professor books like The French Revolution: People Power in Action, Moms Needed Bread!, The Marquis de Lafayette and The Storming of the Bastille.

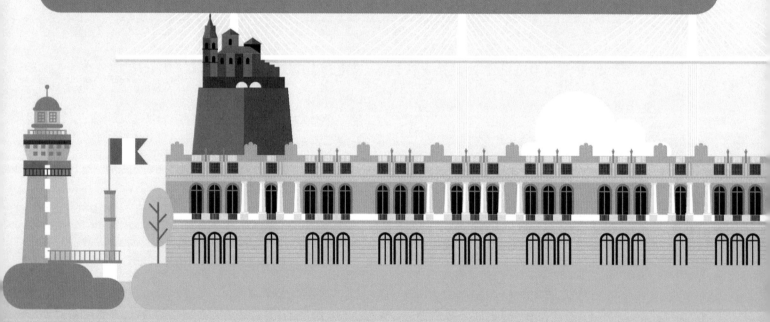